Easy Grammar Plus

Student Test Booklet

Wanda C. Phillips

PUBLISHED BY *Easy Grammar Systems*

SCOTTSDALE, ARIZONA 85255

© 2007

TABLE OF CONTENTS

TESTS

Name_____   **PRE-ASSESSMENT**

Date_____

A. Clauses:
Directions: Place **DC** if the words form a dependent clause; place **IC** if the words form an independent clause. Write **No** if the words do not form any type of clause.

1. _____   After you buy your ticket.

2. _____   After dinner at a fast-food restaurant.

3. _____   After we finish, let's make popsicles.

4. _____   The team flew to Los Angeles after the game.

B. Sentences, Fragments, and Run-Ons:
Directions: Write **S** if the words form a sentence. Write **F** if the words form a fragment. Write **R-O** if the words form a run-on.

1. _____   Lana doesn't like kiwis, she prefers pineapples.

2. _____   Stop.

3. _____   When their parents went to a neighborhood party.

4. _____   Within two hours of hearing about the flood, rescuers responded.

5. _____   Kira drove to the airport, parked, went to ticketing, but she had left her purse in her truck and had to return to it and so she missed her flight.

C. Sentence Types:
Directions: Place correct punctuation at the end of each sentence and write the sentence type on the line.

1. _____   Is Tamarindo in Costa Rica

2. _____   Yikes! We're lost

3. _____   Please remain quiet

4. _____   They live on Shell Avenue   1

D. Business Letters:
   Directions: Label the boldfaced part of this business letter *and* punctuate the salutation (greeting) correctly.

September 21, 20—

Easy Grammar Systems
Post Office Box 100   _____
Scottsdale, AZ   85255

Dear Mr. Phipps

E. Capitalization:
   Directions: Write a capital letter above any word that should be capitalized.

1. have governor t. loon and those from the house of representatives met today?

2. in the summer, they like to eat fish tacos at a mexican restaurant on shell beach.

3. the oldest african-american church was started in the east in 1813 by peter spencer.

4. he studied french history, reading, and biology 101 at cambria college in july.

5. the demacane corporation moved just south of pinnacle peak last tuesday.

6. during thanksgiving weekend, both dad and i read <u>strangers from my native land</u>.

7. take ventura freeway north to see hearst castle and to attend the templeton grape festival.

8. his brother, a banker, speaks japanese and flies to asia on thailand airlines.

9. a delaware company that worked with nasa is located on moonwalker road.

10. did james cook claim the hawaiian islands for the british empire?

11. some pioneers left new england to settle near the salt river in the arizona territory.

12. does the university of virginia foundation run the boar's head inn?

F. Punctuation:
   Directions: Insert needed punctuation.

1. His address is 10 South Street Austin TX 78705

2. Joys aunt a teacher bought a newly remodeled home

3. On May 24 2006 they were married in a small country chapel

2

4. Emma asked   Tate do you need an old branding iron

5. Yes I want to see the movie entitled Struck Twice by Lightning

6. During the last week of September we went to Alaska said Kim

7. Yeah Emily exclaimed My race is next

8. Although Allen is a nurse hes interested in doctors rights

9. Fight Against Bacteria is an article in the magazine entitled Health World

10. The town built the following a childrens hospital a large park and a zoo

11. The team will leave at noon and the band will follow within two hours

12. By the way are you going with us to Missoula Montana next fall

13. The fair is next week however I cant attend

G. Subjects and Verbs:
Directions: Underline the subject once and the verb or verb phrase twice.
Note: Crossing out prepositional phrases will help you.

1. I have purchased a new watercolor by a Western artist.

2. Did anyone find a cat with long gray fur?

3. Before the basketball game, several players were given extra practice.

4. I am definitely sad about your lost hamster.

5. Your brother shouldn't have gone to the library by himself.

H. Contractions:
Directions: Write the contraction.

1. does not - _____   3. I have - _____   5. have not - _____

2. they are - _____   4. how is - _____   6. you will - _____

I. Subject-Verb Agreement:
Directions: Underline the subject once. Underline the verb that agrees twice.

1. Carmello and Bo (was, were) in Ohio recently.

2. Someone in the last few rows (have, has) a cell phone turned on.

3. The girls with the cute, little beagle puppy (like, likes) to walk him.

4. Neither the ladies nor the man with them (want, wants) dessert.

5. One of the watermelons (is, are) ready to cut.

J. Irregular Verbs:
Directions: Circle the correct verb.

1. Have you (spoke, spoken) to your friends about it?

2. He should not have (did, done) that.

3. Carlo has not ever (ridden, rode) a horse.

4. I may have (ate, eaten) too much.

5. Their alarm clock has (rang, rung) three times.

6. They have (drove, driven) to the coast.

7. Have you (drunk, drank) green tea?

8. A sign must have (fell, fallen) during the storm.

9. The couple has (chosen, chose) a house with an old barn.

10. (Lie, Lay) on the floor by the fire.

11. We should have (took, taken) our dogs to the lake with us.

12. The city of Vancouver was (began, begun) in 1792 by the British.

13. They may have (went, gone) to a baseball game.

14. I should have (brung, brang, brought) my camera.

15. Have Mr. and Mrs. Cole (flew, flown) to Dover?

16. The sleepy child had (laid, lain) on the floor.

17. The church's stained-glass window was (broken, broke).

18. That shovel must have (frozen, froze) in the snow.

19. Many doctors must have (came, come) to the conference late.

20. (Sit, Set) beside me!

21. I (saw, seen) him at the mall.

22. Many horses have (ran, run) in that famous race.

23. A reporter had (wrote, written) about the lost diamond mine.

4

K. Tenses:
  Directions: Underline the subject once and the verb or verb phrase twice. Write the tense in the blank.

1. _____ I am leaving soon.

2. _____ I left early.

3. _____ They had left for New York City at noon.

4. _____ Chase will leave on vacation next week.

5. _____ Abigail always leaves food on her plate.

L. Common and Proper Nouns:
  Directions: Place a ✓ if the noun is abstract.

1. ___ jar   2. ___ respect   3. ___ promise   4. ___ air

M. Singular and Plural Nouns:
  Directions: Write the correct spelling of each plural noun.

1. loss - _____   6. display - _____

2. wrench - _____   7. excitement - _____

3. leaf - _____   8. potato - _____

4. robbery- _____   9. badge- _____

5. deer - _____   10. chief - _____

N. Possessive Nouns:
  Directions: Write the possessive in each blank.

1. a cart used by more than one workman - _____

2. a market set up by more than one farmer- _____

3. a home belonging to Tom and Lori- _____

4. computers owned by a company - _____

5. a playroom used by more than one child - _____

O. Identifying Nouns:
  Directions: Circle any nouns.

1. Many strong winds blow through this village and its meadows and into a deep cave.

P. Usage and Knowledge:

1. Circle the correct answer: Josh did the sanding (himself, hisself).

2. Write an interjection: _____

3. Write a gerund: _____

4. Write the antecedent of the possessive pronoun:

      Someone shouted his name over a loudspeaker. _____

5. Circle a reflexive pronoun: We did it ourselves, and nobody helped!

Q. Identifying Adjectives:
      Directions: Circle any adjective.

1. One glossy photograph had French swans on a very lovely lake.

R. Degrees of Adjectives:
      Directions: Circle the correct answer.

1. The road by my cousin's house is the (curvier, curviest) one in the county.

2. She is the (more talkative, most talkative) twin.

3. This shell feels (rougher, roughest) than that one.

4. Of the entire family, Tara seems (more timid, most timid, timider, timidest).

S. Adverbs:
      Directions: Circle the correct answer.

1. You did (good, well).

2. I don't feel (good, well).

3. Ron hardly ever has (no, any) extra change.

4. You are speaking too (loud, loudly).

5. She doesn't know (anybody, nobody) in her new school.

6. Their truck runs (good, well).

T. Identifying Adverbs:
      Directions: Circle any adverbs.

1. Tammy and her sister always play so nicely together.

6

U. Degrees of Adverbs:
   Directions: Circle the correct answer.

1.   Of the two girls, Ellen jumps (farther, farthest).

2.   Mia wins (more often, most often, oftener, oftenest) than her friend.

3.   The injured player walked (more lightly, most lightly) on his right foot.

4.   The dog barked (more ferociously, most ferociously) at the third car.

5.   Bo played (worse, worser, worst, worsest) during the second game.

W. Pronouns:
   Directions: Circle the correct answer.

1.   Pam and (she, her) donated blood.

2.   (Who, Whom) did you call?

3.   The flowers were for Sara and (I, me).

4.   (Them, Those) cookies are too hard.

5.   One of the girls left (her, their) books by the bench.

6.   The coach and (we, us) practiced dribbling.

7.   (Me and my friend, My friend and I, My friend and me) will help.

8.   Annie and (they, them) walked to the ice cream shop.

9.   The first one to present an award was (he, him).

10.   Lance will call (we, us) boys after dinner.

11.   Our cousins are (they, them) with the sheep dog.

12.   The leader handed (she, her) a large manila envelope.

13.   (Who, Whom) has a colored pencil?

14.   Both of the street sweepers ate (his, their) snacks.

15.   The winners are Nat and (me, I).

16.   The debate was between Karen and (he, him).

17.   Please give (they, them) my message.

W. Nouns and Pronouns Used as Subjects, Direct Objects, Indirect Objects, Objects of the Preposition, and Predicate Nominatives:

Directions: Look at the boldfaced word and decide how it is used in the sentence. Write **S.** for subject, **D.O.** for direct object, **I.O.** for indirect object, **O.P.** for object of the preposition, and **P.N.** for predicate nominative.

1. _____ Quit bothering **me**!

2. _____ Their **grandparents** live in Florida.

3. _____ Jenny always earns **money** for her school clothes.

4. _____ Tad became a **bricklayer**.

5. _____ Stay away from the **alley**.

6. _____ Give the **waiter** a tip.

Name_____   **PREPOSITION**
                                            TEST
Date_____

Directions: Cross out any prepositional phrases. Underline the subject once
              and the verb/verb phrase twice.

1.   One of the men leaned against the door during the discussion.

2.   Several dogs at the veterinarian's office were lying by their owners' feet.

3.   Kerry stood in the rain and waited along with the other bus riders.

4.   After the accident, a policeman walked toward the damaged car.

5.   Claude and his aunt live near the park on Houston Avenue.

6.   Before the school carnival, many students carried chairs into a tent.

7.   His nearest neighbor lives across the field and past some water tanks.

8.   Please place this poster regarding water safety above the door.

9.   You may not go outside without your coat, hat, and boots.

10. Throughout the spring, nine robins played underneath our willow tree.

11. A model stood among the ladies and instructed them about proper nutrition.

12. Some horses were running around in the field between the barn and the house.

13. Everyone but the tall man in the blue wool suit remained for the banquet.

14. After the meeting, Mom and her friend will help with refreshments until nine
     o'clock.

15. Large dogs like shepherds and retrievers aren't allowed within the gated area.

Name_____   **VERB TEST**

Date_____

A.   Directions: Write each contraction.

1.   they will - _____   12.   do not - _____

2.   I am - _____   13.   I shall - _____

3.   it is - _____   14.   cannot - _____

4.   was not - _____   15.   we are - _____

5.   you are - _____   16.   is not - _____

6.   she would - _____   17.   who is - _____

7.   could not - _____   18.   does not - _____

8.   will not - _____   19.   here is - _____

9.   they are - _____   20.   I have - _____

10.   you will - _____   21.   are not - _____

11.   she is - _____   22.   we are - _____

B.   Directions: Circle the correct verb.

1.   Juan has (saw, seen) the Hope Diamond.

2.   She (teached, taught) us how to dive properly.

3.   The balls were (thrown, threw) into the center of the ring.

4.   This mop has been (shook, shaken) several times.

5.   Her mother must have (come, came) by to see her today.

6.   Herbs were (grown, grew) in a box on the window sill.

7.   The Harrison family may have (went, gone) water skiing.

8.   They should have (rode, ridden) their bikes in the rain.

9.   Jenny has (swam, swum) since her first birthday.

10.   Have you ever (broke, broken) a bone?

C. Directions: Circle the correct verb.

1. Have you (laid, lain) on the bed very long?

2. If you would have asked, I would have (gave, given) you a key.

3. Each of the choir members has (sung, sang) a solo this year.

4. Was the fireman (took, taken) to the hospital for smoke inhalation?

5. Several of the bubbles had (burst, bursted) on the wand.

6. His answers were (written, wrote) in black ink.

7. The welder has (brung, brought) two torches with him.

8. His mother may have (spoke, spoken) to the coach about his injury.

9. Many hot dogs were (ate, eaten) by the hungry hikers.

10. The candle must have been (blew, blown) out.

11. I should have (risen, rose) earlier than nine o'clock.

12. Sandy could not have (drunk, drank) another ounce of soda.

13. That racer has (ran, run) the mile faster than his opponents.

14. That traveler will have (driven, drove) a thousand miles by the end of her trip.

15. All of the towels were (shook, shaken) and placed on the line to dry.

16. Have the boys and girls (done, did) the scenery for the play?

17. George Washington was (swore, sworn) into office in New York City.

18. This jacket must have (fell, fallen) on the dirty cement.

19. Many pizzas had been (froze, frozen) for the victory celebration.

20. Octopi are (known, knew) by their long, slender tentacles.

21. The baseball player had (stole, stolen) home during the last inning.

22. The Eastern team had (beat, beaten) the Western one in the playoffs.

23. Her jacket had been (torn, tore) by a bush with large thorns.

24. A lady has (bought, boughten) several ceramic giraffes.

25. Their family has (went, gone) to the circus.

D.   Directions: Circle the verb that agrees with the subject.

1.   Sponges (is, are) a type of invertebrates.

2.   A few loons (swim, swims) on that lake each day.

3.   A kindergartner (walk, walks) with her father to school each day.

4.   Each of the divers (perform, performs) three dives in the competition.

5.   Several ranchers (meets, meet) each week to discuss plans for a town barbecue.

6.   A woman with a pretty smile (greet, greets) us at church each week.

7.   Pam's grandfathers (builds, build) vacation cabins in the mountains.

8.   Everyone of the club members (attend, attends) at least three meetings a year.

9.   Freda or her mother (take, takes) the dog for a walk each morning.

E.   Directions: Cross out any prepositional phrases. Underline the subject once
                    the verb/verb phrase twice. In the space provided, write the tense:
                    *present, past, future, present perfect, past perfect, future perfect,
                    present progressive, past progressive,* or *future progressive.*

1.   _____ The boys were yelling to their friends.

2.   _____ Patrick hit the baseball past second base.

3.   _____ One carpenter had forgotten his tools.

4.   _____ By March, she will have saved twenty dollars.

5.   _____ Has anyone brought a drink for the picnic?

6.   _____ A dance student is buying new ballet shoes.

7.   _____ Their brother plays in a sandbox daily.

8.   _____ Will those senators be meeting next week?

9.   _____ Miss Lee will make a decision about moving.

F.   Directions: Cross out any prepositional phrases.   Underline the subject
                    once and the verb/verb phrase twice.   Label any direct object-<u>D.O.</u>

1.   Her dog is (sitting, setting) by her mother.

2.   Have you (laid, lain) this blanket here?

3.   Each person (rose, raised) his hand to vote.

4.   Is the cat (lying, laying) near the litter box?

5.   A toddler (lay, laid) down on a couch to sleep.

6.   Miss Lasko (raises, rises) late on Saturdays.

7.   (Sit, Set) this plate on the table.

8.   Everyone in the arena (rose, raised) to sing the national anthem.

9.   (Sit, Set) in the last row.

G.   Directions: Cross out any prepositional phrases.   Underline the subject once
                    and the verb/verb phrase twice. In the space provided, write <u>L</u> if
                    the verb is linking and <u>A</u> if the verb shows action.

1.   _____   Jonas's hamster eats special food.

2.   _____   Dino tasted some cheesy Greek pie.

3.   _____   Kami bowled a nearly perfect game.

4.   _____   This bun became hard after three days.

5.   _____   Your fresh fudge seems too soft to cut.

6.   _____   Several children skated on a pond.

7.   _____   Yancy became an engineer.

8.   _____   Mrs. Korb is staying with her mother.

9.   _____   The child seemed eager to learn to skate.

14

H. Directions: Cross out any prepositional phrases. Underline the subject once
              and the verb/verb phrase twice. Write the helping (auxiliary) verb(s)
              in the first column and the main verb in the second column.

HELPING VERB(S)   **MAIN VERB**

1. I shall find a way.   _____ _____

2. Should Bo come with us?   _____ _____

3. He may have gone to a baseball
    game.   _____ _____

4. Several watermelons are lying
    near the fence in the garden.   _____ _____

5. That booth was constructed by
    high school seniors.   _____ _____

6. Someone in that city can win
    a trip to Alaska.   _____ _____

I. Directions: Cross out any prepositional phrases. Underline the subject once
              and the verb/verb phrase twice.

1. Mr. Swanson might be going to Canada soon.

2. Have you taken your guitar to the music store for repair?

3. Several rare birds had been seen within a few hours.

4. Before the wedding, the groom must have become very nervous.

5. One of the robins has built a nest in the pine tree.

6. Connie will not be driving to her grandmother's house alone.

7. Can you understand the problem between the two boys?

8. Would you be interested in a ticket to an amusement park?

Directions: Cross out any prepositional phrases.   Underline the subject once
              and the verb/verb phrase twice.

1.   During the game's final seconds, a basketball player made a basket from mid-
     court.

2.   Everyone of the hot air balloons rose early in the moist morning.

3.   The horse and its rider continued to meander down the dusty road.

4.   Many bats had flown out of the cave after the storm at sundown.

5.   Beyond that mountain is a lush green valley about ten square miles in area.

6.   All calves but the one near its mother ambled over to the fence.

7.   Kathryn cannot go to the beach without sunblock and her beach umbrella.

8.   Clay's paper concerning rabies has been placed underneath some books on
     his desk.

9.   Toward the end of the tour, the choir will be traveling through small Swiss
     villages.

10. Mrs. Kempler and her son ski before dinner nearly every day except Sunday.

11. In the lot across from the park, several volunteers planted flowers among some
     tall trees.

12. Please place these within the manila envelopes and address them, too.

13. Throughout the game, the goalie does not play beyond that point.

14. The statue inside the new history museum looks like their Uncle Anthony.

15. The small jet took off within ten minutes of its arrival at Scottsdale Airport.

Name_____   **NOUN TEST**

Date_____

A. Directions: Write <u>C</u> if the word is a concrete noun; write <u>A</u> if the word is an
    abstract noun.

1. _____ wisdom   3. _____ air   5. _____ happiness
2. _____ lion   4. _____ shutter   6. _____ microscope

B. Write <u>C</u> for common; write <u>P</u> for proper.

1. _____ AIRPLANE   4. _____ ADAMS COUNTY

2. _____ JET   5. _____ WASHINGTON, D.C.

3. _____ FUNDWAY AIRLINES   6. _____ SKATER

C. Directions: Write <u>N</u> if the boldfaced word serves as a noun; write <u>A</u> if the
    boldfaced word serves as an adjective. Write <u>V</u> if the boldfaced
    word serves as a verb.

1. _____ Does she **park** her car there every night?
2. _____ In the spring, the residents enjoy the **park**.
3. _____ Those **park** lights are too bright.
4. _____ "I'd like **cream** for my coffee," said Mr. Barnet.
5. _____ To make these cookies, **cream** butter and sugar together first.
6. _____ A white **cream** sauce is used as a base for this soup.

D. Directions: Write the possessive and the word it owns.

1. a computer belonging to Tate: _____

2. skis belonging to three girls: _____

3. a restroom for more than one man: _____

4. brushes belonging to James: _____

5. a project belonging to two students: _____

E.   Directions: In the space provided, write <u>PN</u> if the boldfaced noun serves as a predicate nominative, <u>D.O.</u> if the boldfaced noun serves as a direct object, and <u>I.O.</u> if the boldfaced noun serves as an indirect object. If the noun serves as an appositive, write <u>APP.</u> in the space.

1.   _____   The first shape on the page is a **triangle**.

2.   _____   Mr. Carlson, his soccer **coach**, talked to the team about sportsmanship.

3.   _____   Marge always sends post **cards** to her cousin.

4.   _____   The tailor made **Fred** a pin-striped suit.

5.   _____   The third United States President was **Jefferson**.

6.   _____   Please take your **belongings** with you.

7.   _____   Trish handed the mail **lady** a large envelope.

F.   Directions: Write the plural of each noun.

1.   crepe - _____   5.   decoy - _____

2.   octopus - _____   6.   berry - _____

3.   crash - _____   7.   cross - _____

4.   fez - _____   8.   branch - _____

G.   Directions: First, circle any determiner in the sentence. Then, box any noun following a determiner. Next, reread the sentence and box any other noun(s) in the sentence.

1.   Some bats will be flying from that cave after sundown.

2.   Has Earl's cousin purchased a brick home across from the new library?

3.   The ladies' club gave two scholarships to those women returning for a college degree.

4.   No money was given to my sister for an expedition to Africa in the spring.

5.   Our grandmother is known for her wisdom concerning many matters.

6.   Their family went to Lake Powell, a beautiful body of water in northern Arizona.

7.   Todd and I watched a monkey chase its partner.

20

A.   Directions: Cross out any prepositional phrases. Underline the subject once
                 and the verb/verb phrase twice.

1.   All band members, but William and Iva, will be playing in the concert.

2.   A huge basket of flowers has been placed upon the dining room table.

3.   Keep your shoes with the rubber soles in the laundry room.

4.   During the storm, a group of children stayed inside to play.

5.   Gregg and I planted flowers between a low wall and our house.

B.   Directions: Write the contraction.

1.   I have - _____   3.   what is - _____   5.   I would - _____

2.   could not - _____   4.   they are - _____   6.   will not - _____

C.   Directions: Write <u>L</u> if the verb is linking; write <u>A</u> if the verb is action.

1.   _____   The cook tastes all of her soups.

2.   _____   After the lights went out, we felt our way down the hallway.

3.   _____   Mrs. Fox has become a business owner.

4.   _____   In January, the weather is usually very cold.

D.   Directions: Write the correct form of the verb in the space provided.

(to break)   1.   Her wrist had been _____ in the fall.

(to take)   2.   Lasagna _____ much time to prepare.

(to hang)   3.   Several trousers were _____ in the closet.

(to ride)   4.   He has _____ his horse for an hour.

(to swim) 5. The athlete had _____ the English Channel.

(to be) 6. Your behavior has _____ outstanding.

(to drink) 7. Several gallons of water had been _____ by the thirsty workers.

(to talk) 8. Both the coach and her assistant often _____ with the team.

(to come) 9. Several surfers had _____ to the beach before dawn.

(to go) 10. Jim and Annie had _____ to a car derby.

(to send) 11. That company _____ catalogs to its customers.

(to lie) 12. Many beach visitors had _____ quietly watching the ocean.

E. Directions: Cross out any prepositional phrases. Underline the subject once and the verb/verb phrase twice. On the space provided, write the tense: *present, past, future, present perfect, past perfect, future perfect, present progressive, past progressive,* or *future progressive.*

1. _____ I am waiting for the next bus.

2. _____ The letter from Aunt Sue arrived before noon.

3. _____ Those boots are in great shape.

4. _____ By the end of the month, he will have written forty checks.

F. Directions: Cross out any prepositional phrases. Underline the subject once and the verb/verb phrase twice.

1. A petition concerning zoning was passed around the neighborhood.

2. I shall not have to leave until Wednesday.

3. Go toward your opponent but move outside his reach.

4. This plate should have been placed under the fancy saucers.

5. Are the travelers going through many tunnels during their time in Switzerland?

Name_____   **ADJECTIVE TEST**

Date_____

A. Directions: Write the proper adjective and the noun it modifies in the space
                  provided.

1. Have you been to a maryland beach?   _____

2. Aren wants a horizon television.   _____

3. Do you like mooby chocolate milk?   _____

4. A platter of french toast was served.   _____

5. "I enjoy mexican food," said Miguel.   _____

6. Cameo's choir is planning a european tour. _____

7. Some hawaiian sunsets are colorful.   _____

B. Directions: Write the predicate adjective and the noun it modifies in the space
                  provided. If there is no predicate adjective in the sentence, write
                  <u>none</u> on the line.

1. The head nurse appears upset.   _____

2. Your antique quilt looks new.   _____

3. These stones feel sharp to my feet.   _____

4. Her gift was a beautiful red shawl.   _____

5. The girl remained calm during her speech. _____

6. This lemon pie tastes quite tangy.   _____

7. The picnickers remained in a quiet spot.   _____

8. A worker grew tired in the midday heat.   _____

C. Directions: Choose the correct adjective form.

1. Mt. Everest is (taller, tallest) than Mt. Fuji.

2. Is Lake Superior the (deeper, deepest) lake in the world?

3. Austrid is the (more intelligent, most intelligent) person I know.

4. Was your rafting trip the (more daring, most daring) one you've ever taken?

5. Mrs. Parks is the (nicer, nicest) of the two helpers.

6. Which of these three worms is (longer, longest)?

7. The wedding cake chosen by Cynthia was (larger, largest) than the one selected by her fiance.

D. Directions: Circle any adjectives.

Suggestion: Read each sentence carefully. Circle any limiting adjectives. Then, circle any descriptive adjectives.

1. Two warm bran muffins and orange juice were part of the appetizing breakfast.

2. This tall street light with pink frosted panes serves as an easy landmark.

3. Has Jerome's great uncle visited the covered bridges of the New England states?

4. A cream-filled chocolate eclair with whipped cream topping was the main dessert.

5. Sarah's youngest son had ridden his mountain bike on that spring outing.

6. Several small children were petting a few comical, fluffy puppies.

7. These were the warmest leather boots in the entire shoe store.

8. An American flag was flying at their local post office.

9. Our favorite restaurant is a Chinese one in lower Manhattan.

10. Many flowering cherry trees bloom each year in our nation's capital.

Name_____   **CUMULATIVE TEST**
                                             Adjective Unit
Date_____

A. Directions: Fill in the blank.

1. An example of an abstract noun is _____.

2. An example of a common noun is _____.

3. An example of an interjection is _____.

4. An example of a proper adjective is _____.

5. A word that ends a prepositional phrase is called an _____.

B. Directions: Write the plural of the following nouns.

1. cinch - _____   4. burglar - _____   7. buoy - _____

2. fungus - _____   5. grocery - _____   8. ox - _____

3. paste - _____   6. starfish - _____   9. sister-in-law - _____

C. Directions: Write the contraction.

1. she is - _____   3. cannot - _____   5. you are - _____

2. should not - _____   4. is not - _____   6. had not - _____

D. Directions: Write <u>A</u> if the boldfaced word serves as an adjective; write <u>N</u> if the
                  boldfaced word serves as a noun. Write <u>V</u> if the boldfaced word
                  serves as a verb.

1. _____   This **light** fixture is dirty.
2. _____   Please turn on a **light**.
3. _____   Please **light** the candles.
4. _____   Janice **skates** on her neighbor's pond.
5. _____   Place those **skates** in the closet.

E. Directions: Write fifty prepositions.

1. _____	14. _____	27. _____	40. _____
2. _____	15. _____	28. _____	41. _____
3. _____	16. _____	29. _____	42. _____
4. _____	17. _____	30. _____	43. _____
5. _____	18. _____	31. _____	44. _____
6. _____	19. _____	32. _____	45. _____
7. _____	20. _____	33. _____	46. _____
8. _____	21. _____	34. _____	47. _____
9. _____	22. _____	35. _____	48. _____
10. _____	23. _____	36. _____	49. _____
11. _____	24. _____	37. _____	50. _____
12. _____	25. _____	38. _____	
13. _____	26. _____	39. _____	

F. Directions: Cross out any prepositional phrases. Underline the subject once
and the verb/verb phrase twice. Label any direct object -D.O.; label
any indirect object - I.O.

1. Everyone of the girls on the softball team must carry her own equipment.

2. Frank and his best friend will be going to Baltimore and Annapolis in the spring.

3. Please give your mother this recipe for hot cross buns.

4. Throughout the year, several girls met at Mrs. Polk's house to discuss field day.

5. Has your dentist given you information about a new type of toothbrush?

26

G. Directions: Write the correct verb form in the space provided.

(to choose) 1. Has the group _____ its leader?

(to do)   2. The dishes must be _____ soon.

(to sink)   3. Her toes have _____ into the mud.

(to ring)   4. The tardy bell had _____.

(to see)   5. You should have _____ the look on his face.

(to give)   6. We were _____ several mush balls.

(to drink)   7. Have you ever _____ mineral water?

(to take)   8. Campaign posters were _____ down immediately after the election.

(to bring)   9. Jack has _____ along his dog.

(to part)   10. Whitney had _____ her hair in the middle.

H. Directions: Circle the correct possessive:

1. Several (lady's, ladies') hats were on sale.
2. The (children's, childrens') playground is rather small.
3. One (boy's, boys') picture had been hung on the wall.
4. An award was presented to the (city's, citys') mayor.
5. Some (wasp's, wasps') hives were in a palm tree.

I. Directions: Circle any adjectives.

Suggestion: **First, circle any limiting adjective(s) in a sentence. Then, circle any descriptive adjective(s).**

1. That triangle has three equal sides.
2. A few dogs with pretty bows on their ears left the groomer's work area.
3. Sixteen tourists rode a double-decker bus through several London streets.
4. A small, furry animal darted in front of their speeding car.

J. Directions: Write the tense of the verb in the space provided.

(present of *to eat*) 1. This hamster _____ very little.

(future of *to fly*) 2. We _____ a kite on a windy day.

(past perfect of *to learn*) 3. Jonah _____ early.

(present progressive of *to go*) 4. Nelly _____ to a gym.

K. Directions: Box any nouns.

Suggestion: Identifying adjectives helps to locate most nouns.

1. An unusual computer is sitting on a card table in the middle of their kitchen.

2. In most cases, that attorney speaks to his new client in a private office.

3. In Germany, my father and I visited one castle, several vineyards, and a lake.

4. Will you help Mr. Kirk with this bushel of apples and those sacks of potatoes?

L. Directions: Write <u>APP.</u> if the boldfaced noun serves as an appositive, <u>D.O.</u> if the boldfaced word serves as a direct object, and <u>PN</u> if the boldfaced word serves as a predicate nominative.

1. _____ I have lost a coin, a **dime**.
2. _____ The winner of a free basket of goodies is **Mrs. Larkins**.
3. _____ Throughout the day, the dog chewed his new **bone**.
4. _____ Give Jason a **copy** of that advertisement.

M. Directions: Circle the correct verb.

1. Several chickens (live, lives) in that barn.
2. A customer (sat, set) her purse on the glass counter.
3. The child (lay, laid) on his stomach to watch television.
4. Benny's aunt and uncle (work, works) at a grocery store.
5. Neither my mother nor my sisters (want, wants) another cat.

Name_____   **ADVERB TEST**

Date_____

A. Directions: Write the adverb form of each word.

1. easy -   _____

2. foolish -   _____

3. nervous -   _____

4. fast -   _____

5. final -   _____

6. sudden -   _____

7. good -   _____

8. recent -   _____

B. Directions: Cross out any prepositional phrases. Underline the subject once and verb/verb phrase twice. Circle any adverbs.

1. Quickly he grabbed the fire extinguisher from above the fireplace.

2. Please remove the tiles in the family room very carefully.

3. Shanna hit the ball hard during her first practice.

4. A waitress usually works fast during dinner hour.

5. You can swim underneath the water so well.

6. He answered all questions courteously and confidently.

7. We need to work together on this project concerning recycling.

8. A plumber could not come immediately.

9. You are always quite friendly and act agreeably.

10. One of the penguins padded quite swiftly to the water's edge.

C.   Directions: Write **good** or **well** in the space provided.

1.   His exams went _____.

2.   This is a _____ way to tie a double knot.

3.   You are doing _____ ; keep it up!

4.   Miss Jansen doesn't feel _____ today.

5.   Oprah swims very _____ for a beginner.

D.   Directions: Circle the correct answer.

1.   This frisbee flies (gooder, better) than that one.

2.   Of the triplets, Tiffany sings (more beautifully, most beautifully).

3.   Sweeping the kitchen takes (longer, longest) of all the chores.

4.   My sister walks (more slowly, most slowly) to school than from school.

5.   Jana hits the ball (harder, hardest) of the entire team.

6.   To avoid a collision, the first car stopped (more abruptly, most abruptly) of the four.

E.   Directions: Circle the correct answer.

1.   Mark doesn't have (no, any) ride to the store.

2.   I don't want (any, none).

3.   Kenneth has (no, any) hobby.

4.   She scarcely has (any, no) time to play.

5.   The hamster hardly eats (anything, nothing).

6.   You never want (anybody, nobody) to help you.

30

A. Directions: Circle any abstract noun.

    fin   fan   fist   fun   friend   female   fort   fence   faith   freedom

B. Directions: Write the plural of each noun.

1. proof - _____   4. calf - _____   7. mother-in-law_____

2. ash - _____   5. tissue - _____   8. derby - _____

3. ploy - _____   6. tooth - _____

C. Directions: Write the contraction.

1. should not - _____   3. it is - _____   5. they are - _____

2. we will - _____   4. you are - _____   6. I would - _____

D. Directions: Write <u>A</u> if the boldfaced word serves as an adjective; write <u>V</u> if the bold
                faced word serves as a verb. Write <u>N</u> if the boldfaced word serves as
                a noun.

1. _____ She attended a **flute** recital.

2. _____ Is the **flute** an expensive instrument?

3. _____ Did you **flute** the edges of the pie?

E. Directions: Cross out any prepositional phrases. Underline the subject once and
                the verb/verb phase twice. Label any direct object-<u>D.O.</u> Label any
                indirect object-<u>I.O.</u>

1. Most of the guests signed the register.

2. At the end of the seminar, books were sold at various booths.

3. Kelly baked the class brownies for her birthday.

F. Directions: Cross out any prepositional phrases. Underline the subject once and
           the verb/verb phrase twice.

1. Kimberly wouldn't ride her horse in the rodeo parade.

2. After sunrise, a group of men played golf for several hours.

3. Those ladies and their sons will be attending a banquet at our church.

4. Take these along with you, and wear them after your shower.

G. Directions: If the boldfaced noun serves as an appositive, write APP. in the space.
           If the boldfaced noun serves as a direct object, write D.O. in the space.
           If the boldfaced noun serves as a predicate nominative, write PN in
           the space.

Remember: You need a proof for a predicate nominative.

1. _____ Their cousin, **Ella**, attends a junior college.

2. _____ Our new neighbor is **Adam Jones**.

3. _____ The car door hit **Frankie** in the back.

H. Directions: Fill in the blank.

1. Write a proper noun.   _____

2. Write a proper adjective.   _____

3. Write a phrase.   _____

I. Directions: Write the sentence type.

1. _____   Where have you put the stapler?

2. _____   My answer is final.

3. _____   Please stop that.

4. _____   The train is moving!

J.   Directions: Circle the correct adjective form.

1.   This is the (funnier, funniest) show I have seen.

2.   Jody's published copy was (better, best) than her rough draft.

3.   Her reaction was (more pleasant, pleasanter) than I expected.

4.   Of all the science projects, yours was the (more interesting, most interesting).

5.   Of the triplets, Julie is (more creative, most creative).

K.   Directions: Circle the correct verb.

1.   The policeman (rose, raised) his hand to tell the driver to stop.

2.   One of the truckers (wear, wears) a blue uniform.

3.   Have you (chose, chosen) a different route for the detour?

4.   The baby may have (drank, drunk) a full six ounces of milk.

5.   A bracelet is (laying, lying) on the floor.

6.   Has the chemist (gave, given) us the test results?

7.   Few workers (is, are) taking a break early.

8.   We should have (brought, brang) our jackets.

9.   The jurist must have (took, taken) a newspaper along.

10.   One of the dogs (eat, eats) the other's food.

11.   The key chain and an extra key (was, were) on the desk.

12.   A visitor must have been (sitting, setting) in that empty seat.

13.   Have you ever (wrote, written) your name backwards?

14.   (Lie, Lay) your tiles for the board game on the table.

15.   Mr. and Mrs. Dobson (leaves, leave) early each morning.

L. Directions: Write the possessive form.

1. a yard sale belonging to two families - _____

2. notes belonging to a speaker - _____

3. a clothing store for more than one man - _____

M. Directions: Circle any adjectives.

1. Several blue helium balloons are attached to that long metal pole.

N. Directions: Box any nouns.

1. I must take two boxes of mystery books to the library during the afternoon.

O. Directions: Write P if the group of words is a phrase; write C if the group of words
             is a clause.

1. _____   Down the street.   3. _____   Running through the hall.
2. _____   After James left.   4. _____   Claude has a new hamster.

P. Directions: Write the tense.

1. _____   His grandfather goes to bed early.
2. _____   Have you washed your hair today?
3. _____   Are you planning a surprise party?

Q. Directions: Write S if the group of words is a sentence. Write F if the group of
             words is a fragment. Write R-O if the group of words is a run-on.

1. _____   The batter struck out, but he ran to first base anyway.
2. _____   Melinda rides to the store, her friend always walks.
3. _____   Driving a truck to pick up a load of hay.

R. Directions: Fill in the blank.

1. **Wow! We almost won!** What part of speech is Wow!? _____

2. **Are you chewing gum?** The verb phrase is _____. The

    main verb is _____.

3. **The little boy and girl painted Peter a picture.** Peter is the _____

Name_____   **PRONOUN TEST**

Date_____

A. Directions: Circle the correct pronoun.

1. (Who, Whom) wants to ride a roller coaster?

2. The managers are (them, they) standing by the door.

3. A chef gave (us, we) a lesson in chopping food.

4. (Me, I) intend to explore a cave soon.

5. Her friend writes to (her, she) nearly every week.

6. May (we, us) boys play now?

7. This discussion will remain between you and (I, me).

8. To (who, whom) did you give a hamburger?

9. Our dentist gives (we, us) patients a toothbrush.

10. The librarian told (he, him) to work more quietly.

B. Directions: Write P in the blank if the boldfaced word serves as a pronoun;
                  write A in the blank if the boldfaced word serves as an adjective.

1. _____   **Which** do you want?
2. _____   Are **those** yours?
3. _____   **What** time is it?
4. _____   **That** golf cart is broken.
5. _____   **Each** must carry his own gear.

C. Directions: Circle the correct word.

1. (Their, They're) dog is loose again.
2. I believe (you're, your) right!
3. (It's, Its) going to be very cloudy today.
4. A turtle turned (it's, its) head slowly from side to side.
5. Please ask if (their, they're) dad is coming to get them.

D. Directions: Circle the correct pronoun.

1. Madge gave Shanna and (he, him) several popsicles.

2. Judy and (I, me) noticed a flaw in the sweater.

3. Both want (his, their) dinners late.

4. The explorers and (we, us) want to visit Carlsbad Caverns.

5. Harry and (they, them) might be going to Acapulco.

6. The last people chosen were Karen and (we, us).

E. Directions: Write the antecedent of the boldfaced word.

1. _____   A small insect spread **its** wings.

2. _____   Marcus's farm set is **his** favorite toy.

3. _____   The men looked at **their** boss's schedule to determine if they had to work on Tuesday.

4. _____   One of the boys left **his** books.

5. _____   Joanna and her mother love **their** exercise machines.

F. Directions: Tell how the boldfaced pronoun functions in the sentence.

A. subject   B. direct object   C. indirect object
D. object of the preposition   E. predicate nominative

1. _____   The first person to arrive at the restaurant was **he**.
2. _____   **They** fly kites on windy days.
3. _____   A bakery made **us** a beautiful orange cake.
4. _____   A lady in charge handed **me** several T-shirts.
5. _____   Has **she** cleaned her carpets?
6. _____   Did **you** understand the directions?
7. _____   A referee threw **him** out of the game.

Date_____

A. Directions: Write <u>P.N.</u> in the space if the boldfaced word serves as a predicate nominative. Write <u>P.A.</u> if the boldfaced word serves as a predicate adjective. Write <u>NO</u> if the boldfaced word does not serve as a predicate nominative or predicate adjective.

1. _____ Your hands look very **chapped**.

2. _____ Miss Liston is my friend's **aunt**.

3. _____ Fran looks for **money** with her metal detector.

4. _____ This **old** coin was used in ancient Rome.

5. _____ My best friend is **she** in the blue dress.

B. Directions: Circle the correct adverb form.

1. My sister doesn't ever drive (slow, slowly).

2. That first grader writes her name (good, well).

3. The children playing in the water yelled (loud, loudly) to the passing boat driver.

4. His voice rose (sharp, sharply) as he became angrier.

C. Directions: Circle any adverbs.

1. We sometimes go there for lunch.

2. How did you hurt your wrist so badly?

3. A race horse galloped swiftly by.

4. The lady has frantically searched everywhere for the missing money.

5. He dashed in, looked down at his shoes, and began to chuckle softly.

D. Directions: Label any conjunction-<u>Conj.</u>; label any interjection-<u>Intj</u>.

1. Yippee! Mark and Mandy are entering the race!

2. Either Holly or her sister attends college in North Carolina.

3. Hurray! My parents are going to the reunion, but I may go fishing!

E. Directions: Write the sentence type.

1. _____ Stand up.

2. _____ Look at him stand on his head!

3. _____ He is standing on his head.

4. _____ Can you stand on your head?

F. Directions: Write the tense: *present, past, future, present perfect, past perfect, future perfect, present progressive, past progressive, future progressive.*

1. _____ She likes tarantulas.

2. _____ I shall be flying to Denver next month.

3. _____ The child has fallen off a swing.

4. _____ By spring, Ted will have taken all his exams.

5. _____ Mayor Loo greeted the ambassador from Peru.

6. _____ A newspaper was lying by the road.

G. Directions: Write the contraction.

1. I am - _____   3. will not - _____   5. there is - _____

2. you are - _____   4. we are - _____   6. they have - _____

H. Directions: Write <u>A</u> if the noun is abstract; write <u>C</u> if the noun is concrete.

1. ___ kindness   2. ___ salad   3. ___ caution   4. ___ harp   5. ___ joy

I. Directions: Write <u>C</u> if the noun is common; write <u>P</u> if the noun is proper.

1. ___ PLANT   2. ___ GRASS   3. ___ TOWER   4. ___ EIFFEL TOWER

5. ___ OREGON 6. ___ AMERICA 7. ___ ANGEL   8. ___ GABRIEL

38

J. Directions: Write <u>D.O</u>. if the boldfaced word serves as a direct object.
Write <u>I.O</u>. if the boldfaced word serves as an indirect object.
Write <u>APP</u>. if the boldfaced word serves as an appositive.

1. _____ Dad handed **Tammy** an apple for her lunch.

2. _____ Their friend, **Tammy**, is a great seminar speaker.

3. _____ A small child hit **Tammy** on the back with a toy.

K. Directions: Cross out any prepositional phrases. Underline the subject once and the verb/verb phrase twice.

1. Several of the crew members took a break and sat in the shade.

2. A lion with his ears at attention is lying between two trees near a stream.

3. Take this sword to the auditorium for Miss Dormal and Mr. Master.

4. Headlights should have been turned on before the tunnel entrance.

5. Haven't you ever walked through the woods on a cold, crisp winter day?

L. Directions: Circle the correct answer.

1. A (childrens', children's) play area has been added.

2. Has Uncle Marty done that (himself, hisself)?

3. Several (boy's, boys') jackets are on sale.

4. One (lamb's, lambs') mouth seems to be sore.

5. (You're, Your) idea is being considered.

6. Many (skiers', skier's) poles have been slightly bent.

7. (Mrs. Hass, Mrs. Hass's) husband is an orthodontist.

8. The peacock was spreading (it's, its) beautiful tail.

9. Sooner or later, the (women's, womens') club must reach a decision.

M. Directions: Write the plural.

1. lotus - _____   5. pitch - _____

2. nursery - _____   6. son-in-law - _____

3. clay - _____   7. laughter - _____

4. leaf - _____   8. circle - _____

N. Directions: Circle each correct answer.

1. The parade had not (came, come) down the main street.
2. This opening is (narrower, narrowest) of the three.
3. Nancy's grandmother (serves, serve) as our church's greeter.
4. (You're, Your) the person I most respect.
5. The police officer has (rode, ridden) a horse on his beat for several years.
6. The lady with those crying children (is, are) very upset.
7. The man scrubbed the floor (more vigorously, most vigorously) the second time.
8. A zebra and a giraffe often (stand, stands) near a tree in the African meadow.
9. Two year olds frequently want to do things (theirselves, themselves).
10. Have you (brang, brought) a suitcase with you?
11. (Lie, Lay) here beside the fire and get warm.
12. He (sits, sets) under a tree in the park nearly every evening.
13. The pilot must have (went, gone) to the airport already.
14. This matter is between your sister and (I, me).
15. Her father must have (laid, lain) in his recliner all afternoon.
16. Give (we, us) adults a chance to help you.
17. The winner should have been (me, I).
18. Many ribbons have been given to (her, she) for her athletic talent.
19. Everyone must take (their, his) clothes into the laundry room.
20. Several people in the overturned boat had (swam, swum) to the river's bank.
21. When the phone rang, he answered, "This is (he, him)."
22. The light fixture had been (broke, broken) while still in the box.
23. (We, Us) will be meeting with a senator from Kansas.
24. You are much taller than (I, me).

O. Directions: Box any nouns.

1. The desert is a habitat for some snakes and various cacti.

2. I need a package of napkins, some paper plates, and a few straws for our picnic.

3. Lee's aunt is an aspiring violinist; she hopes to play with the Phoenix Symphony.

4. These boxes containing two lamps were sent to the girls' apartment by mistake.

P. Directions: Circle any adjectives.

1. Several beautiful models wore soft, flowing dresses made of imported silk.

2. Five Dalmatian puppies scampered friskily among many shrubs on their back lawn.

3. The Irish countryside is fertile, very green, and scenic in the summer.

4. That man writes funny short stories, Gothic novels, and humorous poetry.

Q. Directions: Read each group of words. Write F for fragment, S for sentence, and R-O for run-on.

1. _____ Having been chosen as the best.
2. _____ Jenny and John have been married a year.
3. _____ Pizza was delivered for dinner, unfortunately, it was cold.
4. _____ During the summer, Brian goes to his grandmother and grandfather's house in Nebraska and loves swimming in a creek by their home and going to the local fairs plus he drives the tractor on their farm.

R. Directions: Circle the correct answer.

1. They feel (happy, happily) about their choice.
2. You painted that wall (quick, quickly).
3. Garth does his job (good, well).
4. Kimberly's mother looks (tired, tiredly) today.
5. He answered the question (weird, weirdly).
6. Of the four sandwiches, the beef one was (more delicious, most delicious).

Name_____   **PUNCTUATION TEST**

Date_____

Directions: Insert needed punctuation.

1. Gails dad lives at 17251 N Palomino Avenue Sedalia CO 80135

2. Edna hasnt your family visited Trafalgar Square Green Park and Barclay Square in London

3. Her father in law is that tall talkative man in the gray jacket said Mrs Somerset

4. Bernard Waber wrote a childrens book entitled Ira Sleeps Over

5. Yuck The two dogs dishes are covered with bits of food and ants are crawling all over the bowls

6. Jason their best friend was born in St Louis Missouri on May 20 1982 at 2 00 P M

7.
                                          5503 East Blair Lane
                                          Peoria Arizona   85345
                                          March 18 20--
    Dear Artie

    The following three will be traveling to summer camp in your van Joshua Peter and Jenny

                                          Sincerely
                                          Patty

8. When Sally went to a ranch for summer vacation she read and loved the poem entitled Stopping by Woods on a Snowy Evening by Robert Frost

9. Jackson Co
    89 W Marilyn Lane
    Metamora Illinois   61548

    Dear Miss Hanna

       Three fourths of the article entitled Ultrasound Toothbrushes was supposed to be continued on page forty five However that part of the article was missing

                                          Very truly yours
                                          Martin S Treubell

Name_____   **CAPITALIZATION TEST**

Date_____

Directions: Write the capital letter above any word that needs to be capitalized.

1. when captain lovell and i visited the south, we saw the savannah river
    and the site of the battle of shiloh, a famous civil war area.

2. they learned spanish, computer science, and algebra 1 at a junior high school.

3. i. geographical locations

    a. rivers

    b. mountains

        1. located in europe

        2. located in north america

4. their grandfather was given a book entitled the prayer of jabez as a father's
    day gift.

5. juan and his polynesian friends attended a play entitled he was with me in
    the den at star theater last saturday.

6. a child with bronchitis was treated at sunset memorial hospital on drye lane.

7. did mayor torris drive across the golden gate bridge when visiting northern
    california last winter?

8. after buying several gifts at swan gift shop, the american tourist boarded a
    concourse airline flight for new york city.

9. "during thanksgiving vacation, mother and aunt kama helped the moon
    valley helpers club teach spanish at largent college," said kalifa.

10.   1882 south breck drive

                              atlanta, georgia 30327

                              january 4, 20—

dear dirk and cochise,

      to travel to grand canyon national park from your home, take the
black canyon freeway to flagstaff, arizona, and turn west.

                              your friend,

                              thang

A. Clauses:
Directions: Place **DC** if the words form a dependent clause; place **IC** if the words form an independent clause. Write **No** if the words do not form any type of clause.

1. _____ After you buy your ticket.

2. _____ After dinner at a fast-food restaurant.

3. _____ After we finish, let's make popsicles.

4. _____ The team flew to Los Angeles after the game.

B. Sentences, Fragments, and Run-Ons:
Directions: Write **S** if the words form a sentence. Write **F** if the words form a fragment. Write **R-O** if the words form a run-on.

1. _____ Lana doesn't like kiwis, she prefers pineapples.

2. _____ Stop.

3. _____ When their parents went to a neighborhood party.

4. _____ Within two hours of hearing about the flood, rescuers responded.

5. _____ Kira drove to the airport, parked, went to ticketing, but she had left her purse in her truck and had to return to it and so she missed her flight.

C. Sentence Types:
Directions: Place correct punctuation at the end of each sentence and write the sentence type on the line.

1. _____ Is Tamarindo in Costa Rica

2. _____ Yikes! We're lost

3. _____ Please remain quiet

4. _____ They live on Shell Avenue

47

D. Business Letters:
   Directions: Label the boldfaced part of this business letter **and** punctuate the salutation (greeting) correctly.

September 21, 20—

Easy Grammar Systems
Post Office Box 100   _____
Scottsdale, AZ 85255

Dear Mr. Phipps

E. Capitalization:
   Directions: Write a capital letter above any word that should be capitalized.

1.   have governor t. loon and those from the house of representatives met today?

2.   in the summer, they like to eat fish tacos at a mexican restaurant on shell beach.

3.   the oldest african-american church was started in the east in 1813 by peter spencer.

4.   he studied french history, reading, and biology 101 at cambria college in july.

5.   the demacane corporation moved just south of pinnacle peak last tuesday.

6.   during thanksgiving weekend, both dad and i read <u>strangers from my native land</u>.

7.   take ventura freeway north to see hearst castle and to attend the templeton grape festival.

8.   his brother, a banker, speaks japanese and flies to asia on thailand airlines.

9.   a delaware company that worked with nasa is located on moonwalker road.

10.   did james cook claim the hawaiian islands for the british empire?

11.   some pioneers left new england to settle near the salt river in the arizona territory.

12.   does the university of virginia foundation run the boar's head inn?

F. Punctuation:
   Directions: Insert needed punctuation.

1.   His address is 10 South Street Austin TX 78705

2.   Joys aunt a teacher bought a newly remodeled home

3.   On May 24 2006 they were married in a small country chapel

4 . Emma asked   Tate do you need an old branding iron

5. Yes I want to see the movie entitled Struck Twice by Lightning

6. During the last week of September we went to Alaska said Kim

7. Yeah Emily exclaimed My race is next

8. Although Allen is a nurse hes interested in doctors rights

9. Fight Against Bacteria is an article in the magazine entitled Health World

10. The town built the following a childrens hospital a large park and a zoo

11. The team will leave at noon and the band will follow within two hours

12. By the way are you going with us to Missoula Montana next fall

13. The fair is next week however I cant attend

G. Subjects and Verbs:
Directions: Underline the subject once and the verb or verb phrase twice.
Note: Crossing out prepositional phrases will help you.

1. I have purchased a new watercolor by a Western artist.

2. Did anyone find a cat with long gray fur?

3. Before the basketball game, several players were given extra practice.

4. I am definitely sad about your lost hamster.

5. Your brother shouldn't have gone to the library by himself.

H. Contractions:
Directions: Write the contraction.

1. does not - _____   3. I have - _____   5. have not - _____
2. they are - _____   4. how is - _____   6. you will - _____

I. Subject-Verb Agreement:
Directions: Underline the subject once. Underline the verb that agrees twice.

1. Carmello and Bo (was, were) in Ohio recently.

2. Someone in the last few rows (have, has) a cell phone turned on.

3. The girls with the cute, little beagle puppy (like, likes) to walk him.

4. Neither the ladies nor the man with them (want, wants) dessert.

5. One of the watermelons (is, are) ready to cut.

J. Irregular Verbs:
   Directions: Circle the correct verb.

1. Have you (spoke, spoken) to your friends about it?
2. He should not have (did, done) that.
3. Carlo has not ever (ridden, rode) a horse.
4. I may have (ate, eaten) too much.
5. Their alarm clock has (rang, rung) three times.
6. They have (drove, driven) to the coast.
7. Have you (drunk, drank) green tea?
8. A sign must have (fell, fallen) during the storm.
9. The couple has (chosen, chose) a house with an old barn.
10. (Lie, Lay) on the floor by the fire.
11. We should have (took, taken) our dogs to the lake with us.
12. The city of Vancouver was (began, begun) in 1792 by the British.
13. They may have (went, gone) to a baseball game.
14. I should have (brung, brang, brought) my camera.
15. Have Mr. and Mrs. Cole (flew, flown) to Dover?
16. The sleepy child had (laid, lain) on the floor.
17. The church's stained-glass window was (broken, broke).
18. That shovel must have (frozen, froze) in the snow.
19. Many doctors must have (came, come) to the conference late.
20. (Sit, Set) beside me!
21. I (saw, seen) him at the mall.
22. Many horses have (ran, run) in that famous race.
23. A reporter had (wrote, written) about the lost diamond mine.

K. Tenses:
   Directions: Underline the subject once and the verb or verb phrase twice. Write the tense in the blank.

1. _____ I am leaving soon.

2. _____ I left early.

3. _____ They had left for New York City at noon.

4. _____ Chase will leave on vacation next week.

5. _____ Abigail always leaves food on her plate.

L. Common and Proper Nouns:
   Directions: Place a ✓ if the noun is abstract.

1. ____ jar   2. ____ respect   3. ____ promise   4. ____ air

M. Singular and Plural Nouns:
   Directions: Write the correct spelling of each plural noun.

1. loss - _____   6. display - _____

2. wrench - _____   7. excitement - _____

3. leaf - _____   8. potato - _____

4. robbery- _____   9 . badge- _____

5. deer - _____   10. chief - _____

N. Possessive Nouns:
   Directions: Write the possessive in each blank.

1. a cart used by more than one workman - _____

2. a market set up by more than one farmer- _____

3. a home belonging to Tom and Lori- _____

4. computers owned by a company - _____

5. a playroom used by more than one child - _____

O. Identifying Nouns:
   Directions: Circle any nouns.

1. Many strong winds blow through this village and its meadows and into a deep cave.

P. Usage and Knowledge:

1. Circle the correct answer: Josh did the sanding (himself, hisself).

2. Write an interjection: _____

3. Write a gerund: _____

4. Write the antecedent of the possessive pronoun:

   Someone shouted his name over a loudspeaker. _____

5. Circle a reflexive pronoun: We did it ourselves, and nobody helped!

Q. Identifying Adjectives:
   Directions: Circle any adjective.

1. One glossy photograph had French swans on a very lovely lake.

R. Degrees of Adjectives:
   Directions: Circle the correct answer.

1. The road by my cousin's house is the (curvier, curviest) one in the county.

2. She is the (more talkative, most talkative) twin.

3. This shell feels (rougher, roughest) than that one.

4. Of the entire family, Tara seems (more timid, most timid, timider, timidest).

S. Adverbs:
   Directions: Circle the correct answer.

1. You did (good, well).

2. I don't feel (good, well).

3. Ron hardly ever has (no, any) extra change.

4. You are speaking too (loud, loudly).

5. She doesn't know (anybody, nobody) in her new school.

6. Their truck runs (good, well).

T. Identifying Adverbs:
   Directions: Circle any adverbs.

1. Tammy and her sister always play so nicely together.

U. Degrees of Adverbs:
    Directions: Circle the correct answer.

1. Of the two girls, Ellen jumps (farther, farthest).

2. Mia wins (more often, most often, oftener, oftenest) than her friend.

3. The injured player walked (more lightly, most lightly) on his right foot.

4. The dog barked (more ferociously, most ferociously) at the third car.

5. Bo played (worse, worser, worst, worsest) during the second game.

W. Pronouns:
    Directions: Circle the correct answer.

1. Pam and (she, her) donated blood.

2. (Who, Whom) did you call?

3. The flowers were for Sara and (I, me).

4. (Them, Those) cookies are too hard.

5. One of the girls left (her, their) books by the bench.

6. The coach and (we, us) practiced dribbling.

7. (Me and my friend, My friend and I, My friend and me) will help.

8. Annie and (they, them) walked to the ice cream shop.

9. The first one to present an award was (he, him).

10. Lance will call (we, us) boys after dinner.

11. Our cousins are (they, them) with the sheep dog.

12. The leader handed (she, her) a large manila envelope.

13. (Who, Whom) has a colored pencil?

14. Both of the street sweepers ate (his, their) snacks.

15. The winners are Nat and (me, I).

16. The debate was between Karen and (he, him).

17. Please give (they, them) my message.

W. Nouns and Pronouns Used as Subjects, Direct Objects, Indirect Objects, Objects of the Preposition, and Predicate Nominatives:

Directions: Look at the boldfaced word and decide how it is used in the sentence. Write **S.** for subject, **D.O.** for direct object, **I.O.** for indirect object, **O.P.** for object of the preposition, and **P.N.** for predicate nominative.

1. _____ Quit bothering **me**!

2. _____ Their **grandparents** live in Florida.

3. _____ Jenny always earns **money** for her school clothes.

4. _____ Tad became a **bricklayer**.

5. _____ Stay away from the **alley**.

6. _____ Give the **waiter** a tip.

Reflections

Preposition Test

_____

_____

_____

_____

_____

_____

_____

_____

_____

_____

_____

_____

Reflections

Verb Test

_____

_____

_____

_____

_____

_____

_____

_____

_____

_____

_____

_____

Reflections

Noun Test

_____

_____

_____

_____

_____

_____

_____

_____

_____

_____

_____

Reflections

Adjective Test

_____

_____

_____

_____

_____

_____

_____

_____

_____

_____

_____

_____

Reflections

Adverb Test

_____

_____

_____

_____

_____

_____

_____

_____

_____

_____

_____

_____

Reflections

Pronoun Test

_____

_____

_____

_____

_____

_____

_____

_____

_____

_____

_____